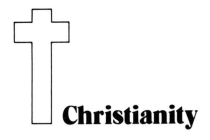 **Christianity**

A First Book

IRENE CUMMING KLEEBERG

Christianity

Franklin Watts
New York, London, 1976

ACKNOWLEDGMENTS
Many people have helped me with this book. Spe-
cifically, I would like to thank David C. Gross,
author and editor and formerly executive vice-presi-
dent of the Jewish Publication Society of America,
and John Stratton, professor of philosophy, Ryerson
Polytechnic Institute, Toronto, for their advice on
specific questions.   *Irene Cumming Kleeberg*

All biblical quotations in this book
are from the King James version

Photographs courtesy of: Religious News Service:
frontispiece; ENIT, Italian Government Travel
Office: pp. 9, 10; F.W.I.: p. 5; The Metropolitan
Museum of Art, Gift of Felix M. Warburg and his
Family, 1941: p. 11; French Cultural Services: p.
15; Library of Congress: pp. 26, 38, 53, 59; French
Embassy Press and Information Division: pp. 28,
30, 31, 41, 52; Rare Book Division, The New York
Public Library, Astor, Lenox and Tilden Founda-
tions: p. 34; The New York Public Library Picture
Collection: pp. 37, 48; United Press International:
pp. 45, 65, 69, 70, 71, 72; American Baptist Churches
International Ministries: p. 55; The Salvation
Army: p. 60. *Cover by One + One Studio.*

Library of Congress Cataloging in Publication Data

Kleeberg, Irene Cumming.
    Christianity.

    (A First book)
    Bibliography: p.
    Includes index.
    SUMMARY: Traces the history of Christianity
from the time of Jesus to the present, and discusses
the major Christian beliefs and holidays, individual
Protestant denominations, and trends in modern
Christianity.
    1. Church history — Juvenile literature. 2. Sects
— Juvenile literature. [1. Church history. 2. Sects]
I. Title.
BR151.K53   270   75-37743
ISBN 0-531-00843-6

Contents

What Is Christianity?
1

The Life of Jesus
4

*Other Christian Events
and Beliefs*
13

*The Early Spread
of Christianity*
19

The Early Christian Church
21

The Middle Ages
25

*Martin Luther and
the Protestant Reformation*
36

Post-Reformation Christianity
43

Protestant Religions
47

*New Religions in
the United States*
62

*Current Trends
in Christianity*
67

*Calendar of the
Western Christian Year*
75

*Brief Chronology
of Christian
Church History*
77

*Membership of
Major American
Christian Groups*
79

Glossary
80

*Suggestions for
Further Reading*
84

Index
85

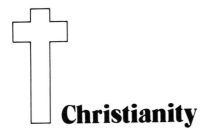

Christianity

What is Christianity?

Christianity is the religion of most people in North, Central, and South America, and in Europe, Australia, and New Zealand. It's an important religion in Asia and Africa, too.

But it is difficult to define Christianty.

There are hundreds of different Christian groups. These are called *denominations*. Even so, all these groups consider themselves Christians.

What do they have in common?

COMMON CHRISTIAN BELIEFS

The main thing Christians have in common is belief in God and belief that Jesus of Nazareth is both the son of God and the *Messiah*, the savior promised to the Jewish people by God. (The Greek word "Christ" means the same as the Hebrew word "Messiah.") The life of Christ and his teachings are central to all branches of Christianity. Christians believe Jesus rose from the dead and gave people the promise of eternal life.

Christians also have the Bible — a book of sacred writings — in common. The Christian Bible is divided into two halves. The first half is often called the Hebrew Bible since most of it was originally written in Hebrew. It is a collection of the sacred writings of the Jewish people. Most Christians call this section the Old Testament. Christians call the second half of the Bible the New Testament. It was written in Greek, the language of educated people at the time.

Christians have divided the Bible into these two sections to emphasize what they see as the change in God's relationship with humans between the Old Testament and the birth, life, and death of Jesus.

Many Christian groups stress that Christianity is a religion of love. They feel that one of the most important parts of the Bible is where Jesus is quoted as saying, when asked what was the greatest commandment, "Thou shalt love the Lord thy God with all thy heart, and with all thy soul, and with all thy mind. This is the first and great commandment. And the second is like unto it, Thou shalt love thy neighbor as thyself." (Matthew 22:37-39)

THE BEGINNINGS
OF CHRISTIANITY

How did Christianity begin?

To answer this question we have to understand something about the political situation at the time of the birth of Jesus in the part of the world then known as Judea, Samaria, and Galilee — now Israel.

This area was part of the Roman Empire and was ruled by the Romans. Before then it had been part of the ancient Jewish land of Israel.

The Jews believed that Moses, with God's guidance, had led them into Israel after they had been slaves in Egypt. They called it the Promised Land and believed that it was a gift to them from God. They resented the rule of their Promised Land by the Romans, and longed for independence.

JEWISH-ROMAN RELATIONS

The Jews were able to live fairly peacefully with the Romans. They were allowed to practice their religion provided they didn't encourage rebellion against Rome. Many Jews were waiting for the Messiah, foretold in various books in the Bible. The belief in a Messiah helped the Jews endure oppression. Many Jews believed the Messiah would be a military leader who would free them from Roman domination and this belief gave them hope.

The Life of Jesus

Toward the end of the first quarter of the first century A.D. Jesus of Nazareth, a man about thirty years old, began to preach to the Jewish people.

He gathered *disciples* (followers), also called *apostles*, and spoke about God. According to the Bible, he also performed miracles. He preached for a short time — three years at the most — and at the end of that time he was put to death.

How do we know?

Although there is some mention of Jesus in other early writings, the most important source for information about his life, teachings, and death is in the New Testament, the second half of the Christian Bible. Scholars believe that Jesus was a real person although they do not always agree on details of his life.

THE GOSPELS

The first four books of the New Testament, Matthew, Mark, Luke, and John, tell the story of the life of Jesus. They are called *gospels,* a word that means "good news."

Mark is the shortest of the four gospels. This gospel doesn't begin with the story of the birth of Jesus — the Christmas story — but with the story of another man, named John, who baptised people. He is often called John the Baptist.

*In this print Jesus is shown
healing sick people.*

Baptism has become an important part of the Christian religion. It is a ceremonial washing, meant to show that the old life, with the old sins, is being washed away. Most Christian religions now practice infant baptism. Babies are baptised by having water poured over or touched to their heads to show that they are Christians and to wash away *Original Sin* — the guilt which, Christians believe, all people must carry because Adam and Eve sinned. According to the Bible, Adam and Eve were the first human beings. Some branches of Christianity baptise only adults.

John the Baptist baptised adults and he probably baptised by immersion — putting the entire person under water.

John preached he was preparing the way for a greater religious leader who would follow him, but many people said that John was the Messiah.

Jesus came to John and was baptised. Then, after spending a period of time alone praying and thinking about his future, Jesus began to preach.

THE PREACHING
OF JESUS

As he preached, he picked up followers, called disciples or apostles, until he had twelve who worked closely with him. And he did more than preach, the Bible says. He also performed miracles and forgave sins.

Jesus usually preached with *parables,* or little stories that were easy to understand. Most of the parables illustrated his message of love for both God and other people.

One day, the Bible says, he preached a very simple sermon

on a mountain, called the Sermon on the Mount. Here is part of the sermon, as recorded in Matthew:

> *"Blessed are the poor in spirit: for theirs is the kingdom of heaven.*
>
> *"Blessed are they that mourn: for they shall be comforted.*
>
> *"Blessed are the meek: for they shall inherit the earth.*
>
> *"Blessed are they which do hunger and thirst after righteousness: for they shall be filled.*
>
> *"Blessed are the merciful: for they shall obtain mercy.*
>
> *"Blessed are the pure in heart: for they shall see God.*
>
> *"Blessed are the peacemakers: for they shall be called the children of God."*
>
> (Matthew 5: 3-9)

OPPOSITION TO JESUS

As time went on, opposition developed to Jesus for both political and religious reasons.

The Romans were worried by Jesus. Wherever he went to preach, huge crowds followed him.

The king of the Jews at this time was appointed by the Romans. He is called Herod in the New Testament. When he heard people saying John the Baptist was the Messiah, he had him executed. He was afraid of Jesus, too, and wanted him to die.

The Jewish leadership felt his religious teachings were false and were *blasphemy* (a crime against God). Many men before Jesus had claimed to be the Messiah.

This meant Jesus had three strong groups of opponents — the Romans, Herod, and the Jewish leadership.

[7]

THE LAST SUPPER

And so we come to the death of Jesus.

It took place during Passover, the celebration of the Jews' escape from slavery in Egypt. It is a very religious time in Judaism.

When Jesus was alive as many Jews as possible went to Jerusalem during Passover for a service of thanksgiving in the Temple.

The Romans, Herod, and the Jewish leaders felt they must get rid of Jesus. He was simply too dangerous.

On the first night of Passover, during the *seder* — the ceremonial dinner which is still part of the Jewish Passover celebration — Jesus spoke to his disciples. He probably realized he would be put to death soon. Christians believe he was telling them how to commemorate him. This seder is called the *Last Supper.*

Two things are part of every Passover meal — *matzah* and wine. Matzah, a bread made without yeast or baking powder, is eaten because when the Jews fled from Egypt they didn't have time to wait for their bread to rise.

Jesus took the matzah, said a blessing over it, and broke it into pieces to pass to his disciples. While he did this he said, "Take, eat: this is my body." He also blessed the wine and passed that around, saying, "This is my blood of the new testament, which is shed for many."

This seder has become a very important part of the Christian religion. Today, it is known as the *Eucharist,* the *Lord's Supper, Communion,* or the *Mass,* and it is the most holy service in many Christian churches.

This painting of the Last Supper is made up of three panels (called a triptych). The artist, Pietro Lorenzetti, lived during the early Renaissance.

These two Crucifixion scenes are very different.
It is interesting to notice that the later work
(an engraving by the Dutch artist Rembrandt
made in the seventeenth century) does not
have any angels in it. The painting (above) is
Italian and dates from the fifteenth century

TRIAL OF JESUS

Jesus and his disciples were in Jerusalem secretly because they knew he was in danger. The Bible says, however, that the Jewish leaders got one disciple (Judas Iscariot) to say where he was.

They arrested Jesus and put him on trial. They asked him if he was the Messiah. He said he was, and since they didn't believe him and felt he was committing blasphemy, they ordered him condemned to death.

The Jewish leaders consulted the Roman officials on any serious matter. In this case they had to get approval of the death sentence from Pontius Pilate, the local Roman governor. He questioned Jesus and finally agreed with their decision and arranged to have Jesus executed.

Jesus was nailed to a cross, or *crucified*. This was the usual Roman method of killing criminals. He died, but the Bible says that instead of staying dead, he rose again. That is, he came back to life on the third day after his death.

Other Christian Events and Beliefs

There are many other events important to Christians recorded in the Bible. These include the birth of Jesus, the visits of the shepherds and the wise men, the ascent of Jesus into heaven, and the events that occurred on the Feast of Pentecost. All these are commemorated by most Christians with their own specific holy days every year. The Christian year begins with *Advent,* a time of preparation for the Christmas celebration.

THE CHRISTMAS STORY

One day, the Bible says, an angel appeared to the young girl Mary, telling her she would have a son. The angel said that God, in the form of the Holy Ghost (or Spirit), would be the father.

Later the Romans decided to take a census. To do this, the local people were required to go to the town from which their families had originally come. Joseph, to whom the pregnant Mary was engaged, went to Bethlehem — David's city — because he was a descendent of David, a great Jewish king.

When they got to Bethlehem they found the city very crowded. The virgin Mary had her baby and was forced to put him in a *manger* (a trough from which cattle eat hay) since there was "no room for them in the inn."

SHEPHERDS AND WISE MEN

The Bible tells that shepherds were watching their sheep on a hillside near Bethlehem. They saw an angel who told them of the birth of Jesus. The first angel was joined by other angels who said, "Glory to God in the highest, and on earth peace, good will toward men."

Wise men — probably astronomers, at that time also astrologers — saw a star and followed it. They believed that this star announced the birth of the king of the Jews and followed it to Jerusalem from their homes in, the Bible says, "the East."

When the wise men got to Jerusalem, they asked Herod the Great (the father of the Herod who had John the Baptist killed) where they could find the child who was born to be king of the Jews. Since Herod was the king of the Jews, he was upset at hearing of a rival.

He told the wise men he didn't know where the child was but asked them to come back and tell him when they'd found the baby so he, too, could worship him. Actually, the Bible says, he planned to have him killed.

The wise men had a dream saying not to tell him, so once they had found Jesus in Bethlehem and given him gifts, they went home by a route which avoided Jerusalem.

The date of the arrival of the wise men to worship Jesus is an important one in most branches of Christianity. Celebrated twelve days after Christmas Day, it is called *Epiphany* for the Greek word meaning "a showing," since that is the day Jesus was shown to the wise men. The wise men were *Gentiles* (non-Jews). Many Christians believe Epiphany is important be-

Many artists have illustrated
important events in the Christmas story.
This fifteenth-century painting
shows the infant Jesus, with his mother,
Mary, being worshiped by shepherds.

cause it meant that Jesus was for the whole world, not just a Messiah for the Jews.

Although the wise men outsmarted him, Herod the Great had not forgotten. Knowing the Messiah was supposed to be born in Bethlehem, he ordered all boy babies in that area under the age of two years to be put to death. This is commemorated as the Slaughter of the Innocents, Holy Innocents' Day, or Childermas.

Again, a dream saved Jesus. Joseph had a dream telling him to take Mary and Jesus to Egypt and stay there until things were safe. They stayed until Herod had died. Then they went home.

LENT AND EASTER

The next major Christian event in the year is *Lent*. Lent commemorates the time when Jesus went away alone to pray and think before beginning his ministry.

Lent is a time of rededication to Christian beliefs in almost all churches. Because some Christians believe Jesus *fasted* (didn't eat) throughout that time, they give up something they like — usually something to eat — as well.

Lent begins on *Ash Wednesday*, a day of solemn prayer. In some churches, ashes are placed on worshipers' foreheads as a sign of penance for sins. Lent ends on *Holy Saturday*, the last day of *Holy Week*, the week before Easter. *Holy Thursday* commemorates the Last Supper, *Good Friday* commemorates the day of Jesus' death on the cross (the Crucifixion), and *Easter*, on Sunday, commemorates the day he rose from the dead (the *Resurrection*).

[16]

ASCENSION AND PENTECOST

Following Jesus' resurrection on Easter, he moved around and among his disciples, staying with them, the Bible says, until what is now celebrated as *Ascension Day*, when he rose directly to heaven.

Those are the important events in the life of Jesus celebrated by most Christians. Another important date, not during Jesus' life, is the *Feast of Pentecost* (Whitsunday).

The disciples had met together to celebrate the Jewish holiday of *Shavuot*, also called the Feast of Weeks. During their meeting they saw tongues of fire dancing on each other's heads and found they were able to speak languages they didn't know.

The story of Pentecost is found in the book in the Bible called the Acts of the Apostles, and many Christians believe this was the Holy Spirit *consecrating* (dedicating to God) the disciples as the first church leaders.

OTHER CHRISTIAN BELIEFS

With time, many other beliefs developed in Christianity. The early church celebrated the Jewish sabbath — Saturday. Later, Sunday, the day Jesus rose from the dead, became the Christian day for religious observance.

Christianity developed views of heaven and hell. *Purgatory*, a place where penance for sin is paid on the way to heaven, is part of the Roman Catholic belief.

Those who lead a truly Christian life will be rewarded in heaven after death. Hardened sinners, on the other hand, will be punished in hell. Because of heaven and hell, the idea of salvation is important. Christians believe that the death of Jesus can save people from hell.

The Trinity is another Christian belief. *The Trinity* is a term used to express the idea that God appears in three persons — as God the Father (the Jewish God), God the Son (Jesus), and God the Holy Ghost or Holy Spirit (God's spirit in the world) — while remaining one God.

What will happen at the end of the world, or in the *Last Days,* is another area of Christian belief. It is believed that Jesus will come back to earth again as the Bible says he promised to do. This is called the *Second Coming.* At this time he will herald the end of the world and bring the *Day of Judgment.* All people will have to answer for the life they have led and will be rewarded in heaven or punished in hell for eternity.

The Early Spread of Christianity

Christianity didn't come to an end with the death, resurrection, and ascension of Jesus.

In the Acts of the Apostles we read about Peter, a disciple, preaching to crowds of people. We are also told that all the disciples were able to perform miracles just as Jesus had done. Many Christians believe that Jesus appointed Peter the first head of the church before his death.

The preaching of the disciples, their faith, the miracles they performed, and their statement that Jesus had risen from the dead attracted many followers. At that time Christianity was still seen as a form of Judaism rather than as a new and separate religion.

Naturally enough, the Romans — and the Jewish leaders — weren't any more pleased by this than they had been by the preaching of Jesus.

THE IMPORTANCE OF PAUL

An important early Christian was Paul, a converted Jew. He was originally named Saul and had been an enemy of the Christians. The Bible says that one day while Saul was on the road to Damascus, he was dramatically converted to Christianity. He believed and most Christians believe he was converted by Jesus himself. Saul took the Greek name Paul.

It was largely through the efforts of Paul, the converted Jew, that Christianity was brought to the Gentiles — people who were not Jews — while Peter remained in mainly Jewish areas preaching to the Jews.

Many people believe that without Paul and his great enthusiasm it is unlikely Christianity would have ever been more than a branch of Judaism. Paul and several assistants traveled extensively and spread the Christian religion throughout Asia Minor and into Europe. Paul's letters, written back to the churches he founded, appear in the Bible as "Epistles." They are still an important influence on Christian practices.

The Early Christian Church

The history of the Christian church before the fourth century is difficult to discover, as little except religious writings were produced.

What is known, however, is that it became a persecuted church once the Romans decided it was not a branch of Judaism but a new religion.

Disagreements developed in the church over certain religious questions. Eventually, they were settled by meetings, called *councils,* or by direct rulings by church leaders. Beliefs which were not accepted by the church were called *heresies.*

FROM PERSECUTED
TO OFFICIAL RELIGION

Christianity was persecuted by the Romans only during its early days. It became the official religion of the Roman Empire in the fourth century. In 312 Constantine the Great, a contender for the title of emperor, was fighting a battle at Rome.

According to legend, Constantine saw a cross in the sky with the words *In hoc signo vinces* ("In this sign you will conquer") under it. He used the cross to lead him into battle, won the battle, became a Christian, and made Christianity the official religion of the Roman Empire.

Whether or not the story of Constantine's conversion is true is unimportant. What is important is that once converted to Christianity, Constantine used all his power to help spread and protect the religion.

Furthermore, by making Constantinople (renamed from Byzantium) his permanent capital and the "second Rome" he increased the influence and importance of the East and the Eastern Church.

By the year 500 Christianity had become the dominant religion in Syria, Egypt, North Africa, parts of what is now the Soviet Union, the Persian Empire (now Iran), Arabia, Ethiopia, and parts of India.

Many of these countries are no longer Christian because later influences of Islam, Buddhism, and Hinduism destroyed the foothold Christianity had gained.

THE EASTERN ORTHODOX CHURCH

When Constantinople became a capital of the Roman empire, the leader of the church there naturally became more important.

Churches in the East looked to this leader — rather than to the far-away *pope*, or bishop, of Rome — for guidance. There were disagreements for the next seven hundred years as the two churches developed their own distinct characteristics. But the churches did not separate until 1054, when the *patriarch* of the Eastern Orthodox Church excommunicated the pope of the Roman Catholic Church and the pope excommunicated the patriarch. (*Excommunication* suspends a person from church membership.) This is called the *Schism,* a word which comes from a Greek word meaning "split."

In 1453, when Constantinople fell to the Turks, the two churches were further separated, apparently once and for all.

It was not until December 7, 1965, during Vatican Council II, that the two churches took back their mutual excommunications. Still, the Schism has not really been healed.

THE CRUSADES

As time passed, Christianity found itself facing competition in Christian areas from Islam (A.D. 622 is generally considered the date of the founding of Islam). Mohammed, who founded Islam, saw his religion as a total system of government. Moslems fought and conquered — moving across much of the Christian world and converting the inhabitants.

Despite the Schism, many Christians hoped the break between the Eastern Orthodox and Roman Catholic churches was only temporary. At the end of the eleventh century, the Byzantine emperor asked help from the West in defending the Holy Land against the Moslems. The West answered by starting the *Crusades* (holy wars). The response was overwhelming. Not only trained soldiers but many ordinary people volunteered to go fight Islam. While there were many sincere Crusaders, others saw the wars as a chance for adventure and even wealth.

In the end, the Crusades — there were eight major crusades during the eleventh through thirteenth centuries — didn't work. Most of the areas that had been converted to Islam remained Islamic. In addition, the Crusades themselves were a tremendous drain on the West. People resented the expense and the failures of the Crusades, and blamed the church for the loss of lives and money.

When still later Constantinople fell to the Turks and to Islam in 1453, Christianity was at a low point.

The Middle Ages

The term Middle Ages is used to cover the broad period from about A.D. 400 to 1500 in Europe. Naturally, in such a long period of time, there were many changes and it's impossible to say that there was one type of life everywhere.

There are certain themes that ran through the Middle Ages, however, and one of the most important was Christianity. To an extent unknown today, except in Islamic nations, the church and the state were interrelated.

ORDINARY LIFE IN THE MIDDLE AGES

The word *feudal* is often used to describe the way of life during the Middle Ages. This means there were a few large landowners, of limited but great power within their own areas, and a great many extremely poor people, living as peasants and working at least part of the time for these landowners. The only hope that poor people had of escaping from poverty was through the church — the source of education at the time.

Life was not comfortable by our standards, even for landowners. Crops often failed, and Europe was ravaged by plagues which would kill as much as 50 percent of the population. Even keeping warm in cold weather was a problem.

This print shows Clovis I, the first French king to become a Christian. He was baptized into the faith late in the fifth century. The small size of the church in the illustration indicates that Christianity was not yet one of the main influences in France at this time.

Much of the color, pageantry, and pattern of life came from church rituals and celebrations.

The church was the source not only of education but also of culture. Since religion was so important it affected every area of life. Almost all art and music were religious. Literature was mainly religious, too.

The appeal of Christianity to people whose lives were constantly threatened by disease, to people who were not enjoying the life they were living, was essentially in the color it gave to life on earth and the hope it gave for a much better life in heaven after death.

This encouraged certain social customs.

Christianity came to preach that each person was born in life to a certain position and the greatest thing he or she could do was to be content with that life while waiting to get to heaven. This theme became even stronger in later Christianity when the established social order was threatened by revolution, but a thread of it was present in the Middle Ages.

ACHIEVEMENTS OF THE MIDDLE AGES

Many scholars believe that under the leadership of the church, the twelfth and thirteenth centuries saw great achievements. It was during this time that the first universities were started by religious groups. With time, cities began to become important again, and *guilds* (groups of skilled workmen) developed. These city people became quite wealthy independently of the church, leading the church to have mixed feelings about them.

The Cathedral of Notre Dame in Amiens, France.
Construction was begun in A.D. 1220, but the spire
was not completed until the sixteenth century.

On the one hand, the church seemed to feel there was something wrong with the city person's interest in gaining wealth. On the other hand, this same wealth was a source of income for the church, and wealthy city dwellers were encouraged to give generously to the church.

Cathedrals were built in the cities. The medieval cathedrals are thought of as one of the great achievements of the period.

Building the cathedral united the community. Almost everyone contributed, if not with money, then with physical labor. Once built, the cathedral was much more than a place of worship. Government carried out its business inside the cathedrals, many of which were designed so they could hold most of the local population.

THE MONASTIC MOVEMENT

There had always been people in Christianity who felt they must withdraw from the world — the daily life of ordinary people — to be truly holy.

In the Middle Ages, however, their way of life developed into the *monastic* system, the form it usually takes today in Christianity.

Separate monastic groups, usually called *orders*, were formed for both men and women. Monastic life stressed self-denial and combined hours of manual or intellectual work with hours of prayer. Most orders vowed poverty, chastity, and obedience (to the head of the order and through the head to the church as represented by the pope).

France is the birthplace of many famous
religious orders, many of which are still active
today. The monk (at left) and the nuns (above)
continue to follow the traditional way of
life of their medieval forbears in France.

These orders often went to unsettled areas to preach Christianity and found monasteries. Once there, they cleared land for agriculture, leading others — not members of religious orders — to follow them.

The monasteries were the cultural centers for much of the Middle Ages. As the schools founded during the classic Greek and Roman times disappeared, the monks and nuns continued to read and to copy books. The monasteries were the most important places for learning to read and write. Their records are the major source for histories of the period.

In addition to running schools the monasteries also ran orphanages and hospitals. They even provided places for travelers to stay.

It would be wrong to assume that members of religious orders in the Middle Ages always lived up to their ideals. They did not, and many people became critical of the church because of the worldliness of some of the members of these orders.

THE JEWS IN
THE MIDDLE AGES

The relationship between Christians and Jews worsened during the Middle Ages. The threat to Christianity of Islam and the Crusades led to feelings that the Jews were much the same as Moslems.

Jews were also blamed for killing Jesus. They were persecuted for their religion, were forced to convert to Christianity, were martyred, or, at best, were required to live in special areas (later called *ghettos*) and wear special dress.

SAINTS

During the Middle Ages the honoring of *saints* (very holy people) became more important in the life of the church and to the common people. Originally, saints were named more or less by popular opinion. Later, formal systems were set up for their recognition; certain requirements, usually of a miraculous nature, were needed for a person to be *canonized* (declared a saint) by the church.

Mary, the mother of Jesus, became extremely important in the worship of the church. Prayers were addressed to her asking her to mediate with her son.

There are thousands and thousands of saints. Among the important ones of the Middle Ages is Saint Francis of Assisi (born about 1181, died 1226), who started an order stressing poverty and humility. He and his followers lived as wandering preachers, and slept in abandoned churches and leper houses. Saint Francis considered animals, insects, and even death, to be his brothers and sisters.

Saint Benedict (born about 480, died about 547) is known today because of his *rule* (list of regulations) for the communities of monks he founded. This rule is still used in numerous monasteries (both for men and for women) throughout the world.

Saint Catherine of Siena (born about 1347, died 1380), a member of the Dominican order of nuns, was both deeply religious and an advisor to popes. During her lifetime, the increasing worldliness of the church led to rival popes, both claiming supreme power. She fought hard to solve this problem while leading a life of humility.

This late-Medieval woodcut is from
the Poor Man's Bible and shows
scenes from the life of Jesus.

THE END OF
THE MIDDLE AGES

Toward the end of the Middle Ages various influences which had kept the church strong began to lose their strength.

The church suffered from weak leadership and the worldliness of some of its priests and members of religious orders. Some local priests were extremely ignorant.

As discussed, the failure of the Crusades also contributed to a growing disillusionment with the church.

Towns became more important and the people living in them grew less dependent on the church. Learning became more widespread, leading to the questioning of the church.

Finally, the fall of Constantinople in 1453 meant that scholars of Greek and Latin classics moved into Europe, reviving interest in these classics.

These and many other changes helped shape the *Renaissance,* a time of great creativity in the arts and rising individualism. They also influenced the Protestant Reformation.

Martin Luther and the Protestant Reformation

Toward the end of the Middle Ages people became progressively more critical of the Roman Catholic Church. Many resented giving to the church money that would leave their own country and go to Rome.

In addition, the peoples in the different areas of Europe began to be interested in their differences from their neighbors. These people began to feel a need for a religion that did not have allegiance to anyone outside their country.

Many of the people who were dissatisfied with the church wanted to correct its faults from within. They were called *reformers*. There were many reformers before the Protestant Reformation, but because they failed they were labeled heretics.

Finally there came a leader who was strong enough to succeed.

MARTIN LUTHER

This leader was Martin Luther, and he was the first truly successful reformer of the Protestant movement.

Martin Luther, a monk who was educated in law, had been shocked by what he considered the worldliness of the church in Rome when he was sent there by his order. However, it was over the selling of *indulgences* in Saxony, now part of East Germany, that Luther broke with the church.

[36]

Luther lecturing at the
University of Wittenberg

This print shows Martin Luther and Philip Menlanchthon (another German reformer) presenting their religious views to Charles V, the newly elected Holy Roman Emperor. The meeting occurred in 1530 at Augsburg, but Luther himself was not allowed to come since he was already excommunicated. The engraving is not historically accurate.

Indulgence is the term to describe a reduction of the *penance* (punishment) which must be paid for sin. When Martin Luther fought against indulgences, the custom of the church was to sell them for money. A rhyme of the time (translated from the German) was:

"When the coin in the coffer rings,
The soul from Purgatory springs."

Luther felt it was important for this custom to be discussed publicly.

THE NINETY-FIVE THESES

In 1517, Luther made up a list of ninety-five *theses* (theories) concerning indulgences and nailed them to the doors of the town church in Wittenberg, Germany.

The ninety-five theses were widely copied and reported on and acquired support from people who agreed with Luther and felt too much of the wealth of their area was being drained away to Rome.

Later, Luther said the German church should be controlled by Germans, and he believed the common people should be able to read the Bible in their own language — German — instead of in the Latin translation the church used. He added other demands as time went on.

Finally, Rome threatened Luther with excommunication (removal from church membership) if he didn't stop preaching. He refused, was excommunicated, and left the Roman Catholic Church, taking with him many supporters and eventually making the religion he founded — which came to be called Lutheranism — the German state religion. His translation of the Bible into German became the common Bible of the German people.

In the rest of the West the same feelings the Germans had were stirring. The movement Luther launched spread throughout the West, gathering strength from other reformers such as John Calvin.

ROMAN CATHOLIC REFORMS

Following Luther's success, attempts were made to reform the Roman Catholic Church from within. This movement is usually called the *Counter-Reformation.*

The Society of Jesus (the *Jesuits*) was founded, a religious order devoted to spreading Christianity while combating Protestantism. The Jesuits were largely responsible for winning Austria, Poland, the southern Netherlands, and parts of Germany, Bohemia, and Hungary back to the Roman Catholic Church or at least halting the spread of Protestantism.

The popes of the sixteenth century were fairly successful in correcting the major faults of the church. *Simony* (the buying or selling of religious offices, such as that of bishop) was eliminated, standard forms of worship were developed, laws and government were reorganized, and both more education and a more religious life were required of parish priests.

INQUISITIONS AND WAR

The term *Inquisition* refers to groups designed to investigate heresy against the Roman Catholic Church. It became a

*Henry IV of France is leading his troops
into battle in one of the many religious wars
that took place between Protestants and
Roman Catholics. The battle illustrated here
took place in the late sixteenth century.*

powerful and often inhuman tool of the Counter-Reformation.

There were two forms of the Inquisition — one ruled by the church and the other, the Spanish Inquisition, headed by the Spanish rulers. The Spanish was the more severe. People accused of heresy (going against the teachings of the Roman Catholic Church) were tortured and in many cases burned to death.

Many if not most of the wars fought during this period were religious wars between Protestants and Roman Catholics. Both sides have their *martyrs,* people who died for their beliefs.

Post-Reformation Christianity

During the years after the Reformation the Roman Catholic and Protestant churches reviewed their beliefs and governing bodies, and the Protestant movement broke down into additional groups as people worked out their own ideas of what religion should be. We will discuss some of the specific Protestant groups and beliefs later.

During the late eighteenth and throughout the nineteenth centuries movements arose, however, which cut across all parts of Christanity. In addition to the founding of certain specific religions in this period (notably in the United States), the *missionary* movement and the *revivalist,* or evangelical, movement affected Christian thought and history.

THE MISSIONARY MOVEMENT

Christianity, from the time of Paul on, had always had missionaries. Roman Catholic missionaries brought Christianity to the Americas and in many cases also claimed the land for their governments.

The movement gained strength in the nineteenth century among Protestants. In the nineteenth century the Western world, and especially the English-speaking countries, felt responsibility for the rest of the world. They felt that they had an obligation to bring their civilization to what they considered the uncivilized parts of the world.

Governments sent people to such parts of the world as Asia and Africa to colonize these areas, and the churches went, too. The churches sent missionaries who were entrusted with converting the inhabitants to Christianity.

During the nineteenth century this was primarily a Protestant movement, although the Roman Catholic Church did have some missionary orders which became strong at this time.

THE REVIVALIST MOVEMENT

The revivalist movement was strongest in the United States but also important in other countries. Mainly a Protestant movement, it began during the eighteenth century and continues today, but was at its peak during the nineteenth century.

It was one of the periodic attempts Christianity has made throughout history to renew itself. Revivalism had a strong emotional appeal. It stressed such things as *conversion* — a dramatic change in one's life — and, often, public confession of sins or statements of belief.

Revival meetings, held either in churches or in the open air, were enthusiastically attended by entire congregations and often entire towns.

Many Protestant denominations today, rather than have a young person confirm baptismal vows upon reaching maturity, require that the person experience conversion — a de-

Many revivalist groups are active today in the United States. In this photo we see boy evangelist Michael Lord, Jr., preaching to the congregation at the First Church of the Nazarene in Salisbury, North Carolina.

sire to turn away from his or her old life accompanied by a desire to lead a new one (being "born again").

Today, the revivalist or evangelistic tradition is carried on by several Protestant leaders including Billy Graham. Moral Re-Armament is a nonsectarian group in the evangelical tradition.

Protestant Religions

The basis of many Protestant religions is disagreement with Roman Catholic doctrine, past or present. Today, the major disagreement is on the doctrine of the infallibility of the pope, the leader of the Roman Catholic Church, which says that when the pope speaks in his official capacity as leader of the church his statements are always true. Protestants simply do not accept this.

Protestants believe that the Bible, rather than any human being or group of human beings, is the final authority on matters of religion, and that every individual has the right to read and interpret the Bible for himself or herself. They do not believe that a priest is necessary to reach God.

THE SACRAMENTS

The Roman Catholic Church believes that there are seven *sacraments,* or deeply religious ceremonies: baptism, confirmation, the Eucharist or Mass (Communion or the Lord's Supper), penance, *ordination*, marriage, and *Extreme Unction* (anointing with oil people in danger of death).

Protestants believe there are only two sacraments — baptism and Communion. Protestants believe that only these two sacraments were actually established by Jesus.

The Anabaptiſt.　　　　　**The Browniſt.**

The Familiſt.　　　　　**The Papiſt.**

*An unknown seventeenth-century cartoonist
makes fun of the many-sided quarreling
that took place in England among different
Christian groups. We see an Anabaptist,
a Brownist (Congregationalist), a Papist
(Roman Catholic), and a Familist
(member of a mystical Protestant sect
of the day) tossing a Bible in a blanket.*

The Roman Catholic Church preaches the *transubstantiation* of the bread and wine during the Mass. It believes the bread and wine actually become the body and blood of Jesus.

Protestants believe that Jesus' words "This is my body" and "This is my blood" were and are only symbolic. Communion, Protestants believe, commemorates the death of Jesus rather than repeating it.

The sermon is usually very short in the Roman Catholic Church. In most Protestant churches, the sermon is considered central to the service and is quite long.

Although most Protestant churches have these elements in common, different reformers stressed different aspects of the religion. In the rest of this chapter the various Protestant groups will be described.

THE CHURCH OF ENGLAND

The reasons for the Reformation in England were more political than religious. Many people were unhappy with the Roman Catholic Church in England, and attempts at reform had been made before, but the main reason for the break with Rome was Henry VIII's wish to divorce his first wife, Catherine of Aragon. The pope refused to permit the divorce and eventually Henry and most of his people left the Roman Catholic Church. This resulted in the establishment of the *Church of England*, also called the *Anglican* or *Episcopalian* Church.

The service of the Church of England is largely a translation of the Latin Roman Catholic service, although the sermon is more important and *hymns* (religious songs) have been added. The *clergy* play much the same role as in Roman Catholicism.

The *Oxford Movement,* begun in 1833 in the Church of England, introduced more formality to the service, confession to a priest rather than the general confession by the entire congregation, and more interest in saints. Today, those who practice the Anglican religion in this way are called "high" church; those who do not and stress the Protestant side of the religion are called "low."

THE METHODISTS

The Methodists, originally a reform movement within the Church of England, started when a group of students at Oxford led by John and Charles Wesley (usually called the Wesley brothers) and George Whitefield met together for Bible study, prayers, and discussion. They wished to reach out to the lower classes which they felt the Church of England ignored.

The group was called Methodist because the members were considered methodical in their habits.

Methodists stressed and stress the importance of the sermon. Music is important, and Charles Wesley was a gifted writer of hymns. The Wesleys rejected Calvin's idea of predestination in favor of the idea of free will, which teaches that a person's actions can determine his fate (see section on Calvinism in this chapter).

American Negroes, dissatisfied with segregated conditions in the Methodist Church during the nineteenth century, started the African Methodist Episcopal Church and the African Methodist Episcopal Zion Church. (*Episcopal* means "having bishops.") Methodists, including the Negro churches, have split over the years into many groups.

THE CONGREGATIONALISTS

The Congregationalists began as a reaction against the structure of the Roman Catholic and Church of England churches, which stress authority handed down through priests and ministers. Congregationalists were originally called Separatists and considered themselves a Church of England reform. Each local church (*congregation*) decides its own practices and beliefs, since the Congregationalists believe that Jesus Christ himself is the head of each congregation.

CALVINISM

John Calvin, a Swiss, was responsible for the beliefs which at the time of the Reformation started the national Church of Scotland (known today as the Presbyterian Church outside Scotland), the Dutch Reformed Church in the Netherlands and Germany, and the Huguenots in France.

Calvin preached a stern religion. He believed that some people were saved and others doomed — no matter what they do during this life.

This belief, called the *doctrine of predestination*, has caused great controversy; it has been somewhat modified by most present-day churches descended from the Calvinistic tradition.

The early Calvinistic churches believed that one way a person could tell if he was one of the saved was by whether he was successful. Calvin also preached that each individual had a duty to use the gifts he was born with; this concept, with its emphasis on efficiency, hard work, and thrift, is called *the Protestant ethic*.

The clergy are relatively unimportant in the Calvinistic

*Engraved portrait
of John Calvin*

This satirical seventeenth-century print
pokes fun at both the Puritans and the
Anglicans (members of the Church of
England). A famous contemporary rhyme
uses humor and exaggeration to express
the anti-Puritan feelings of the day:
    "To Banbury came I, O profane one
       Where I saw a Puritan — one
       Hanging of his cat on Monday
       For killing of a Mouse on Sunday."

churches (in contrast to their role in the Lutheran and Anglican churches). Calvinist and most Protestant religions have strong laymen's organizations which run the churches or help to run them.

THE PURITANS

Puritanism is the name given to a movement in the sixteenth and seventeenth centuries that started in the Church of England with the aim of purifying it. Puritanism has influenced both the Presbyterian and Congregationalist churches. It was itself strongly influenced by Calvin and stressed predestination. However, most Puritans left the Anglican Church and were called "nonconformists." The Puritans settled New England.

THE PRESBYTERIANS

Presbyterianism is a system of church government based on courts made up of ordained clergy and members of the congregation. The *minister* has the role of preaching, teaching, and administering the sacraments; *elders* run the church with the ministers; *deacons and trustees* handle other matters. The Presbyterian church, both in the United States and in Scotland, where it is the Church of Scotland, has split into many groups.

THE BAPTISTS

The history and beliefs of the Baptists are more difficult to define than that of most other groups. Even before the Reformation there were movements which felt that the only baptism ordained by Jesus was adult baptism. Eventually, the Baptists

Baptists in the United States are still active in missionary work. In this 1975 photo, Louise Paw of the American Baptist Congress is visiting with other Baptists in Zaire, a country in Africa.

came to believe that this baptism must be *immersion* (getting wet all over rather than just the head).

The earliest Baptist group was one of the many reform movements in the Church of England. In the United States, Baptists are the single largest Protestant religion. Baptists have divided into many groups, or *sects*, but they all stress the authority of the Bible and practice adult baptism.

THE LUTHERANS

Lutheranism, the religion founded by Martin Luther, has a modified formal structure with church leaders determining policy. There are Lutheran bishops in Germany and the Scandinavian countries. There are several branches of Lutheranism today, reflecting historic controversies. The role of priests is similar to that in Roman Catholicism.

THE UNITARIANS

The Unitarian religion developed from a belief that there was one God, rather than the threefold Trinity of Father, Son, and Holy Ghost or Spirit taught by most of Christianity. Some other Christian groups feel that Unitarians cannot be considered Christian.

During the nineteenth century over one hundred Congregationalist churches in New England voted themselves out of that religion and into the Unitarian religion. The Unitarian and Universalist (a group with different origins but similar beliefs) churches have recently united.

THE ANABAPTISTS

The Anabaptists were a religious movement both before and during the Protestant Reformation. Martin Luther considered their teachings dangerous.

They believed converts to their religion — even if already baptised — must be rebaptised, and practiced adult baptism. They refused to fight in wars or take oaths.

The Mennonites (occasionally called the Swiss Brethren) are descended from them. Today, the Mennonites have a congregational form of church government and usually stress extremely simple dress.

There are many branches of the Mennonite religion, including the Amish, known for their refusal to adopt many modern developments and insistence on the withdrawal of all members from the modern world, and the Hutterische Community, or Hutterian Brethren, who practice common ownership.

THE FRIENDS

The Society of Friends (*Quakers*) began in England in the 1600s as one of many movements in the Church of England. George Fox, its founder, felt that ceremony kept many away from God. He believed in an extremely personal God who spoke to man through an "inner light."

Most Quaker churches (usually called meetings) do not have ministers or a set service. Instead, when the spirit moves members of the congregation to speak, it is believed God is speaking through them.

Quakers have refused to fight in wars since their founding, with many *conscientious objectors* in the group (people who refuse to fight because their consciences won't permit it).

THE SHAKERS

An offshoot of the Quakers, the Shakers, who settled in the United States in the late eighteenth and early nineteenth centuries, are primarily of historic interest. They believed their leader, Mother Ann Lee, represented the mother element of Christ's spirit.

The movement picked up many members in the nineteenth century, but the demands of chastity for all (no new members were born into the religion) and an insufficient number of new converts are causing it to die out.

THE SALVATION ARMY

The Salvation Army, originally an evangelistic movement which stressed international charity work, was founded by an Englishman named William (and called General) Booth. In contrast to other evangelists who tended to try to renew Christian interest in church members, the Salvation Army reached out to derelicts and other poor people. The Army has always believed in combining physical care — meals, places to sleep — with its religious message.

The Army has special training colleges and women as well as men become officers. No particular beliefs are required to join, although the Army fits in with the evangelical Protestant tradition.

*In this nineteenth-century American engraving,
the Shakers are depicted unfavorably by
the artist. At times the Shakers were persecuted
in the United States, and some members of the
sect were imprisoned for refusing to serve as
soldiers in the Civil War because it was
against their religious beliefs to bear arms.*

Youngsters at a Salvation Army summer camp
enjoy an informal class in botany.

THE MORAVIANS

The Moravians were founded by followers of John Huss, an early (1415) Protestant martyr. Almost wiped out by persecution, the Moravians were finally protected by Count von Zinzendorf in Saxony (now in East Germany) where they settled in 1722. Groups came to the United States and founded settlements including Bethlehem, Pennsylvania, and Salem, North Carolina. John Wesley, a founder of the Methodists, was influenced by the Moravians.

New Religions in the United States

Christianity in the United States is in an unusual position compared to Christianity elsewhere because, once the United States became a nation, there was complete religious freedom.

This freedom made it easier for religions to develop within Christianity. Some of them are described in this chapter.

THE SEVENTH DAY ADVENTISTS

The term *adventists* is used to describe people who expect the Second Coming of Christ soon. At this time it is believed that Jesus will judge people and begin the *millennium* (one thousand years of peace).

The Seventh Day Adventists are descended from a movement founded by William Miller, an American, who believed Christ was coming in 1844. When this didn't happen, many Adventists left the religion.

However, others continued to believe, feeling that Miller's prophecy had been misinterpreted. Special practices include observing Saturday as the Sabbath in the Jewish tradition. It is believed this will help bring the Second Coming. Seventh Day Adventists also avoid eating meat and using narcotics and stimulants.

THE CHURCH OF JESUS CHRIST
OF LATTER DAY SAINTS

The Church of Jesus Christ of Latter Day Saints, also called the Mormons, was founded by Joseph Smith when, Mormons believe, he was given the Book of Mormon on gold tablets in New York State in 1827; their location was shown to him by the Angel Moroni.

Disagreement with the Mormon beliefs and the practice by the Mormons of *polygamy* (marriage to more than one wife at the same time) were somewhat responsible for the intolerance of their neighbors. The group fled to Ohio from New York, then to Missouri, then to Illinois, where Joseph Smith, the prophet, and Hyrum Smith, the patriarch, were murdered.

Brigham Young led the Mormons to what was then the territory and is now the state of Utah, where they established a colony. The group abolished polygamy in 1890.

The Mormons practice adult immersion for baptism and believe that the body survives in heaven after death, with God and the angels having physical bodies. Mormonism teaches that Jesus was a missionary to the Indians in what is now the United States.

The Mormons have a strong missionary program throughout the world and call members of other religions, including Jews and other Christians, Gentiles. The Mormons have divided, with smaller groups disagreeing with the large Utah group.

CHURCH OF CHRIST, SCIENTIST

The Church of Christ, Scientist, was founded in Boston by Mary Baker Eddy, who published her statement of its beliefs,

Science and Health with Key to the Scriptures, in 1875; it was established as a church in Boston in 1879.

This religion teaches that only God is real, that matter is unreal, and that therefore such things as sin, pain, and illness are also unreal. The religion preaches that proper thinking can keep people from experiencing physical illness and can cure it once it does occur.

Christian Scientists believe that vaccination and inoculation are not needed but accept them when demanded by government as they feel they cannot affect a Christian Scientist one way or the other.

JEHOVAH'S WITNESSES

The Watch Tower Bible and Tract Society is better known as the Jehovah's Witnesses. This religion, founded by Charles Taze Russell, stresses belief in the Second Coming of Jesus.

The Jehovah's Witnesses believe in strong missionary work to convert others to the religion. They have no churches or ministers and publish extensively. Since they believe God's kingdom has already arrived on earth, they refuse to show allegiance of any kind to government.

CHRISTIAN CHURCH

The Christian Church was founded as a nonsectarian Protestant group in the early nineteenth century. It drew most of its members from the American frontier. Members like to think of themselves as a brotherhood rather than a church or denomination. The religion grew out of the evangelistic movement

*People who want to become members
of the Jehovah's Witnesses must
be baptized into the faith. This
meeting in Cincinnati a few years ago
took place on a hot July afternoon.*

and also shows some Presbyterian influence. It subsequently broke into several groups.

The Disciples of Christ have a similar history and orientation. Members of both groups call themselves simply "Christians."

Current Trends in Christianity

We have seen that there are many different definitions of Christianity and many different Christian movements.

Today, the various movements, while in most cases still remaining separate, are growing closer to an understanding of each other. For the first time in centuries, there is an attempt to see the common bonds instead of the differences.

This was most dramatically seen at Vatican Council II. Throughout much of its history the Roman Catholic Church has held councils to settle controversial matters and renew the life of the church. These councils are meetings of church leaders.

Vatican Council II, held from 1962 to 1965, changed the Roman Catholic Church in ways which have been far-reaching.

While the most significant results of Vatican Council II were the changes in the Roman Catholic Church, there was also an attempt to reconcile all branches of Christianity. We have already mentioned that the mutual excommunications by the patriarch of the Eastern Orthodox Church and the pope of the Roman Catholic Church, dating from 1054, were taken back during Vatican II. Non-Roman Catholic Christians were invited to attend the council as observers. They had been invited to earlier councils, but they were welcomed at Vatican II and attended.

For Roman Catholics, the most dramatic change has been

in the *liturgy,* or formal church service. Latin, which had been the language of the service from the third century on, has been replaced by the *vernacular* (whatever language is used by the worshippers in their everyday life).

FURTHER EFFECTS
OF VATICAN II

The questioning in the Roman Catholic Church which was expressed at Vatican II has not stopped.

Many Roman Catholics are openly agitating for further change — notably in laws against divorce, against birth control and abortion, and against the marriage of priests. Certain groups of church leaders have produced their own statements of beliefs. Individuals have also taken strong stands against church leaders.

CHANGES IN
PROTESTANTISM

The questions facing Christianity which led to the calling of Vatican II have also led to changes in Protestantism. Many branches of Protestantism have changed their service to make the language more modern.

This questioning has also led to discussion concerning the role of women in the church. In those churches which do not permit women to become ministers, including the Roman Catholic and some Protestant denominations, there is agitation for their acceptance. Other churches which have traditionally permitted women to become ministers are trying to give them greater responsibility.

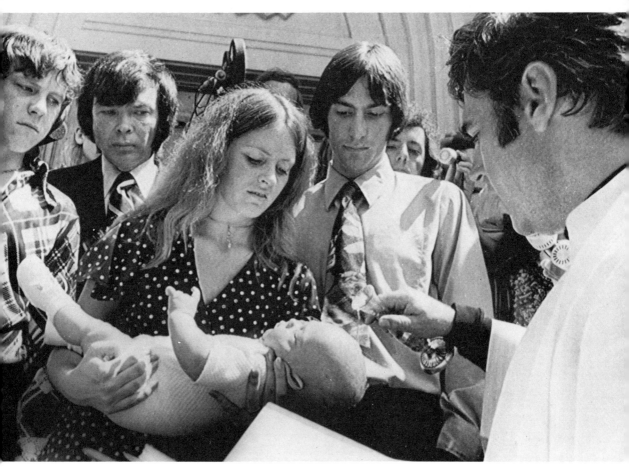

*This three-month-old baby is being baptized
on the steps of the Immaculate Conception
Church in Marlboro, Massachusetts. Local
Catholic officials had refused to allow him to be
christened inside the church because his mother
was in favor of more liberal abortion laws.*

*In 1970 Elizabeth A. Platz was ordained
as the first female Lutheran minister.
She is giving Communion to her mother.*

Three Episcopal priests are celebrating
the Holy Eucharist in the interdenominational
Riverside Church in New York City. In 1974
eleven women were ordained as Episcopal priests
even though the male priest who performed
the ceremonies faced possible dismissal.
When the recently ordained women in this
photograph entered the church, the congregation
welcomed them enthusiastically with applause.

Two Roman Catholic priests, Father Philip Berrigan (left) and Father Daniel Berrigan (right) are burning draft board records. This incident took place in 1968 and was intended as a political protest against United States involvement in the war in Southeast Asia.

POLITICAL ACTION

Although at various times the churches have involved themselves in political questions (during the Civil War several Protestant denominations split along North-South lines), during the first part of the twentieth century most churches and religious leaders held themselves aloof from politics.

This changed during the 1960s, when many churches and church leaders took active roles in urging the extension of civil rights to all citizens and trying to end the war in Southeast Asia.

Today, priests, ministers, and members of religious orders are running for — and winning — political office. Church groups are influencing corporate policy by urging corporations in which they invest to show social responsibility, and many churches are actively working to improve the quality of life for everyone.

Each one of the new trends in Christianity has its opponents.

The reforms of Vatican II have been rejected by some Roman Catholics, who continue to recite the mass in Latin although they have risked the anger of the church in doing so.

THE PENTECOSTAL MOVEMENT

There are several movements in Christianity today which cut across sectarian lines. One of the most significant is the Pentecostal movement, an attempt to re-create in church services the experience the disciples had on the Feast of Pentecost when, the Bible says, tongues of fire danced on their heads and they spoke in *tongues* (languages they didn't know).

The Pentecostal movement has followers in all branches of Christianity, including Protestantism and Roman Catholicism. The Children of God, a small Pentecostal group made up of young people who have left their families, has received a good deal of publicity recently because of the parents' attempts to get their children to come home.

ECUMENISM

The *ecumenical movement* is aimed at reuniting all branches of Christianity in one body. It has received a great deal of attention and is the theoretical aim for most major branches of Christianity, but it would be unrealistic to expect this reunion to occur soon.

However, bit by bit various Protestant denominations, divided from the start by national lines or split later by such causes as the American Civil War, are joining together. Many smaller towns have community churches, Protestant in orientation but otherwise nonsectarian.

For the immediate future the most that can be hoped is that different branches of Christianity will be willing to meet together in brotherhood to consider questions facing Christians. After the bitterness of the centuries among differing Christian groups, this is in itself an important achievement.

Calendar of the Western Christian Year

The major holy days in the Christian year include *Christmas*, celebrating the birth of Jesus, *Good Friday*, commemorating his death, and *Easter*, the day when Christians believe Jesus rose from the dead.

Easter is a "movable feast" — it changes from year to year. The date of Easter affects other dates. The date of Easter in the Eastern Orthodox religion does not always coincide with the date of Easter in Western churches. The ecumenical movement has discussed fixing the date of Easter, with the second Sunday in April often suggested.

The dates of Christmas (December 25) and Epiphany, the day the Wise Men first saw Jesus, do not change.

The following table gives the dates of the movable feasts as now established through the year 1985:

	1977	1978	1979
Ash Wednesday	February 23	February 8	February 28
Good Friday	April 8	April 24	April 13
Easter	April 10	March 26	April 15
Ascension	May 19	May 4	May 22
Pentecost	May 29	May 14	June 1
Advent Sunday	November 27	December 3	November 30

	1980	1981	1982
Ash Wednesday	February 3	March 4	February 24
Good Friday	April 4	April 17	April 9
Easter	April 6	April 19	April 11
Ascension	May 15	May 28	May 20
Pentecost	May 25	June 7	May 30
Advent Sunday	November 30	November 29	November 28

	1983	1984	1985
Ash Wednesday	February 16	March 7	February 20
Good Friday	April 1	April 20	April 5
Easter	April 3	April 22	April 7
Ascension	May 12	May 31	May 16
Pentecost	May 22	June 10	May 26
Advent Sunday	November 27	December 2	December 1

Brief Chronology
of Christian Church History

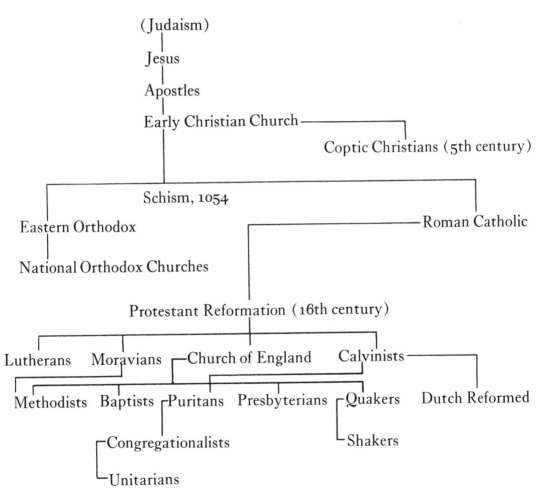

(Judaism)

Jesus

Apostles

Early Christian Church————————————

Coptic Christians (5th century)

Schism, 1054

Eastern Orthodox

Roman Catholic

National Orthodox Churches

Protestant Reformation (16th century)

Lutherans   Moravians   ┌Church of England   Calvinists

Methodists   Baptists ┌Puritans   Presbyterians ┌Quakers   Dutch Reformed

┌Congregationalists

└Unitarians

└Shakers

This chart is designed to show major influential groups in Christianity. Omitted are such groups as the Mormons, Christian Scientists, Seventh Day Adventists, and Jehovah's Witnesses, which are outside the main trends of Christian thought. Also omitted are groups such as the United Church of Canada and other groups resulting from recent Protestant ecumenical movements.

Membership of Major American Christian Groups

Membership figures are difficult to verify and different churches have different ways of counting members. Most Protestant denominations, for instance, include only adult members. Furthermore, some churches consider a person a member even if he or she has not attended the church for some years.

All figures are approximate; many of these churches are divided.

Baptist	27,000,000
Christian Church (Disciples of Christ)	1,300,000
Christian Science	does not reveal membership
Church of Christ	2,400,000
Eastern Orthodox	4,500,000
Friends	70,000
Jehovah's Witnesses	500,000
Lutheran	9,000,000
Mennonite	171,000
Methodist	13,000,000
Moravian	62,000
Mormon	3,400,000
Presbyterian	4,000,000
Protestant Episcopal	3,000,000
Roman Catholic	48,000,000
Seventh Day Adventist	450,000
Unitarian Universalist	200,000

Source: World Almanac; Yearbook of American Churches

✝ Glossary

The following is a listing of words in the text which may be unfamiliar. Words covering a large concept — such as Protestant Reformation — are defined where they are used.

Apostles — The term *apostle* usually refers either to the first twelve followers of Jesus or to successful missionaries, such as Paul.

Ascension — In Christianity, ascension refers to the rising of Jesus to heaven in bodily form after he appeared to his disciples following his resurrection. The Roman Catholic Church believes that Mary, the mother of Jesus, also ascended to heaven with her body.

Baptism — A religiously important ceremony of sprinkling with or immersing in water. In Christianity, it signifies the death of sin and the start of a new life. When infants are baptised, they are also officially named. Certain branches of Christianity, notably the Baptists, baptise only adults.

Blasphemy — Is speaking of God in a nonreligious, sinful way.

Christ — See *Messiah*.

Clergy — People who have been ordained to perform religious duties. See *Ordination*.

Communion — The service commemorating the Last Supper of Jesus during which he blessed bread and wine and told his disciples "This is my body" and "This is my blood." It is the most holy service in most branches of Christianity.

Congregation — A group gathered together for religious worship.

Convert — A person who has turned from his or her old life to a new, religious one. Many Christians believe conversion is brought about by God's influence through the Holy Spirit.

Coptic Christianity — The dominant form of Christianity in Ethiopia and Egypt, it is a pre-Reformation (fifth century) movement labeled a heresy by the Roman Catholic Church.

Council — The Roman Catholic Church calls councils to settle questions and renew religious life. The most recent was Vatican Council II, held from 1962 to 1965.

Crucifixion — The death of Jesus on the cross is central to much of Christianity. Many Christians believe that by this death Jesus atoned for all sin.

Day of Judgment — Christianity teaches that the world will one day come to an end and all people — both living and dead — shall be judged by their lives. On this Day of Judgment it will be decided where each one will spend eternity.

Denomination — Any specific group within the Christian religion, although the term usually refers to Protestant groups.

Disciples — This word, meaning followers, is used of followers of Jesus.

Easter — Easter is the day Christians celebrate the resurrection (rising from the dead) of Jesus.

Ecumenism — The word *ecumenism* describes the ideal of one united Christian church, rather than the many denominations of today.

Eucharist — See *Communion.*

Excommunication — A severe punishment which removes a person from church membership. Literally, it means removal from the right to receive communion.

Fast — To avoid all or some kinds of food.

Gentiles — A word used by Jews to describe all non-Jewish people and by Mormons to describe all non-Mormons.

Heresy — A heresy is an opinion contrary to that of the (usually Roman Catholic) church. Believing a heresy may lead to excommunication.

Indulgence — An indulgence excuses a person from penance for sin.

Last Days — The term Last Days refers to the Second Coming and the Day of Judgment when, some Christians believe, the world shall come to an end.

Last Supper — The last meal Jesus shared with his disciples. It is commemorated in Communion.

Liturgy — The liturgy is the formal, set service used in some branches of Christianity.

The Lord's Supper — See *Communion.*

Martyr — A person who dies, usually violently, for his beliefs.

Mass — See *Communion.*

Messiah — The Messiah is the savior promised to the Jewish people by God. Christians believe Jesus was this Messiah; the Greek word *Christ* means Messiah.

Ordination — Ordination is an official ceremony entitling a person to act as a priest or minister to a group.

Original Sin — The sin with which all people are born because Adam and Eve sinned against God.

Patriarch — The patriarch is the leader of the Eastern Orthodox Church.

Penance — The act of being contrite for sin, confessing it, and being absolved of it, plus some act to atone for the sin.

Pope — The pope is the leader of the Roman Catholic Church.

Resurrection — Most Christians believe that Jesus rose from the dead on Easter Day. This is called the Resurrection.

Schism — From a Greek word meaning split; it usually refers to the break between the Eastern Orthodox and Roman Catholic churches in 1054.

Second Coming — The time when, many Christians believe, Jesus will return to earth. Many also believe this will start the *millennium* (a thousand years of peace) and include the end of the world and the Day of Judgment.

Sect — A religious group which does not agree with the teachings of the main body of which it is a part.

Simony — One of the causes of the Protestant Reformation. It was the buying and selling of religious offices (such as the position of bishop) by the church.

Suggestions for Further Reading

The Bible — At least two translations are recommended — the King James version, first published in 1611, for the beauty of its language, and a modern version for understanding. Modern Bibles include:

Good News for Modern Man, American Bible Society, 1966 — A modern translation of the New Testament.

The Bible, A New Translation, by James Moffatt, Harper & Brothers, New York and London, 1922 — An extremely free translation, including the Old Testament, going further in some respects than many scholars consider justified. It does, however, provide flashes of illumination of otherwise obscure points.

The Bible as History, by Werner Keller, William Morrow and Company, New York, 1956 — A fascinating study of archeological and scientific evidence for biblical writings. Keller's bias in favor of proving the Bible historically correct is clear, but even discounting this, interesting information is provided.

There is little material for young readers which is not biased in one direction or another. Most writings have been designed to stress a particular point of view.

Index

Acts of the Apostles, 17, 19
Advent, 13, 75–76
Adventists, 62
Amish, 57–58
Anabaptists, 57
Anglican Church, 49–50
Apostles, 4, 6, 19, 80
Ascension Day, 17, 75–76, 80
Ash Wednesday, 16, 75–76

Baptism, 6, 47, 54–56, 80
Baptists, 54–56
Benedict, Saint, 33
Bible, 1–2, 4, 20, 40, 47
Booth, William, 58

Calendar, Church, 75
Calvin, John, 40, 50, 51
Calvinism, 50, 51–54
Catherine of Siena, Saint, 33
Childermas, 16
Children of God, 74
Christ. *See* Jesus Christ
Christian Church, 64–66
Christian Scientists, 63–64

Christianity
    official religion of Roman Empire, 21–22
    spread of, 19–20
Christmas, 75
Church, Christian (worldwide)
    chronological history, 77–78
    membership, 79
Church of Christ, Scientist, 63–64
Church of England, 49–50
Church of Jesus Christ of Latter Day Saints, 63
Commandments, 2
Communion, 8, 47–49, 80
Confirmation, 47
Congregationalists, 51
Constantinople, 22–23, 24, 35
Counter-Reformation, 40
Crusades, 23–24

David, 13
Disciples, 4, 6, 19, 81
Disciples of Christ, 66

Easter, 16, 75–76, 81
Eastern Orthodox Church, 22–23, 67

Ecumenism, 74
Eddy, Mary Baker, 63
Epiphany, 14
Episcopalian Church, 49–50
Eucharist, 8, 47, 82
Evangelical movement, 43–46
Extreme Unction, 47

Feasts and festivals, 75–76
Feast of Pentecost, 17
Feast of Weeks, 17
Fox, George, 57
Francis of Assisi, Saint, 33
Friends (Quakers), 57

Good Friday, 16, 75–76
Graham, Billy, 46

Heaven, 17–18
Hell, 17–18
Herod, 7
Holy days, 75–76
Holy Ghost, 13, 18
Holy Innocents' Day, 16
Holy Saturday, 16
Holy Thursday, 16
Holy Week, 16
Huss, John, 61
Hutterische Community, 58

Inquisition, 40–42
Islam, 23

Jehovah's Witnesses, 64
Jesuits, 40

Jesus Christ, 1, 2, 4, 18
    birth, 13
    crucifixion, 12
    opposition to, 7
    preaching of, 6–7
    resurrection of, 16
Jews, 2, 3, 4, 7, 8, 12, 14, 16, 32
John, Saint (the Evangelist), 4
John the Baptist, 4, 6, 7
Joseph, 13, 16
Judaism, 8, 20
Judas Iscariot, 12

Last Supper, 8, 16, 82
Lent, 16
Lord's Supper, 8, 47, 82
Luke, Saint, 4
Luther, Martin, 36–40, 56
Lutheranism, 40, 56

Mark, Saint, 4
Mary, Virgin, 13, 16, 33
Mass, 8, 47, 82
Matthew, Saint, 4, 7
Mennonites, 57
Methodists, 50
Middle Ages, 25–35
Miller, William, 62
Miracles, 4, 6, 19
Missionary movement, 43–44
Mohammed, 23
Monastic groups, 29
Moral Re-Armament, 46
Moravians, 61
Mormons, 63

Moses, 2
Moslems, 23

New Testament, 2, 4

Old Testament, 2
Ordination, 47, 82
Original Sin, 6, 82
Oxford Movement, 50

Passover, 8
Paul, Saint, 19–20
Pentecost, 75–76
Pentecostal movement, 73–74
Persons, of God, three, 18
Peter, Saint, 19
Pontius Pilate, 12
Popes, 40, 47, 83
Predestination, 50, 51
Presbyterianism, 54
Protestant ethic, 51
Protestant Reformation, 35, 36–40
Protestantism, 36–42, 43–46, 47–61,
    68–74
Puritanism, 54

Quakers, 57

Renaissance, 35
Resurrection, 12, 16, 17
Revivalist movement, 43–46
Roman Catholic Church, 22–23, 36,
    67–68
Roman Empire, 2, 3

Sabbath, 17
Sacraments, 47
Saints, 33
Salvation Army, 58
Saul. *See* Paul, Saint
*Science and Health with Key to
    the Scriptures* (Eddy), 63–64
Second Coming, 18, 62, 83
Seder, 8
Separatists, 51
Sermon on the Mount, 7
Seventh Day Adventists, 62
Shakers, 58
Slaughter of the Innocents, 16
Smith, Joseph, 63
Society of Jesus, 40
Spanish Inquisition, 42

Taye, Charles, 64
Trinity, 18

Unitarians, 56
Universalists, 56

Vatican Council II, 67–68

Watch Tower Bible and Tract So-
    ciety, 64
Wesley, Charles, 50
Wesley, John, 50
Whitefield, George, 50
Women, role in church of, 68

Young, Brigham, 63

About the Author

This book grew out of a course Irene Cumming Kleeberg gave on Christianity in a New York City high school, where she found that many young people, both Christian and non-Christian, deeply interested in Christianity, were unable to find information without a doctrinal bias. A longtime student of religion, she is the author of eight books, but this is her first on religion.